PLAYING THE RECORDER

AN ELEMENTARY METHOD WITH A LARGE COLLECTION
OF NEWLY ARRANGED EASY-TO-PLAY PIECES

by Florence White
and Anni Bergman

ALTO

ISBN 978-0-7935-5002-9

EDWARD B.
MARKS MUSIC
COMPANY

EXCLUSIVELY DISTRIBUTED BY
HAL•LEONARD®
CORPORATION
7777 W. BLUEMOUND RD. P.O. BOX 13819 MILWAUKEE, WI 53213

FOREWORD *to the teacher*

The recorder has been widely recognized as an instrument most suitable for beginning music students. Its range is limited, its technical difficulties are at a minimum, and it is therefore possible to concentrate on learning the rudiments of music without the problems that a more difficult instrument presents.

There is one "danger"; the comparative simplicity of the instrument is a temptation to progress too rapidly with resultant confusion, half-learning and frustration. When we teach music to a beginner, especially to a young child, it is extremely important to realize that we introduce him to a new language with all kinds of new and mystifying symbols. The beginner must be sure at every point that he is really learning this new language. We must allow him to familiarize himself with it slowly — as slowly as he needs — even if this means that it will take him a few months to learn four or five tones. It has been our experience that this approach never results in boredom, but rather in a feeling of success and great accomplishment.

In using this approach, the recorder teacher has to collect materials from many sources. *PLAYING THE RECORDER* does this for him by presenting a maximum of good materials at each step in the student's progress, from folk music to old masters. The music teacher should attempt from the first lesson to develop the student's musicianship; that is, to train his ear and musical concepts, his sense of rhythm, his ability to hear, without playing it, the music he sees on the printed page.

We feel that it is advisable to start with an introductory lesson. The teacher should show the student how to hold the recorder, how to blow it in order to get a pleasant tone, how to use the tongue and how to cover the holes with the left hand. In this lesson it is usually possible to teach a simple song such as "Hot Cross Buns" by rote, thereby giving the student a feeling of accomplishment and also encouraging him to experiment with his new instrument.

LESSON I in this book starts with a more formal approach. The book is divided into lessons, but this does not mean that each student's lesson should coincide with a lesson in this method.

The authors wish to express their appreciation to Hilda M. Schuster, Director of the Dalcroze School of Music, for checking the manuscript and making valuable suggestions.

FOREWORD to the student

Look at your recorder. You will find that it has one hole in back. This hole is for the thumb of your left hand. There are seven holes in front; the three top holes are for fingers 1, 2 and 3 of your left hand.*) The four lower holes are for fingers 1, 2, 3 and 4 of your right hand. You will first use the fingers and thumb of your left hand, using the right hand to help you hold your recorder.

You must be sure to cover the holes firmly, using the flat part of your finger tips.

Put the mouthpiece between your lips and blow softly, whispering "tuh" as you blow. Listen carefully to the sound you make. Soon you will learn to hear when you have produced a good, clear tone. If you squeak at first, it will probably mean that you are not covering the holes tightly enough.

In the fingering diagrams, the holes to be covered are filled in; those to be left uncovered are open circles. When two fingerings are given, the first is the German fingering; the second, the English fingering. You will also find alternate fingerings in the text. They are necessary because not all recorders are the same. If you find that one of the fingerings given in the text does not sound in tune, try the alternate fingering.

All music written for the soprano and sopranino recorders sounds one octave higher than the notation.

To take good care of your recorder, keep it as dry as possible and never blow it too hard.

*)

left hand   right hand

13346-48

PLAYING THE RECORDER

LESSON I

When we want to play music, we must know which notes to play and how long to play each note. In order to do this, we must learn the signs and symbols of music writing.

These five lines and four spaces are called the staff: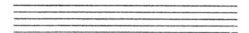

Each of our tones will have a place on the staff, designating the pitch.

This is the G clef sign: it designates which line of the staff is called G.

Our first note is E:

To play **E**, we cover the thumb hole and the first (top) hole of the left hand. To blow a tone, we must use the tongue, saying a light "tuh" as we start each new tone.

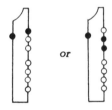

We will play our first tone with three different note values in $\frac{4}{4}$ time:

This is called a time signature. The upper figure tells us the number of beats or counts in each measure. The lower figure gives us the measurement or duration of these beats. In this example, therefore, there are four counts in a measure and each count is equal to a quarter note or its equivalent. The first beat of the measure is the "downbeat", the strongest beat.

The lines running up and down show the measures. They are called bar lines.

Clap and play:
1. Quarter notes. They have one count each:

Count:

2. Half notes. They have two counts each:

Count: 1 2 3 4 1 2 3 4

3. A whole note. It has four counts—a very long note.

Count: 1 2 3 4 1 2 3 4

How many quarter notes equal a half note? A whole note? How many half notes equal a whole note?

Let's change the rhythmic pattern by putting all these note values together Take a breath when you see this sign ,

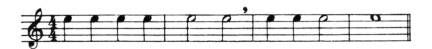

Make up more rhythmic patterns like this.

New Note:

D

Thumb and fingers 1 and 2 of left hand.

Now we have two notes. We vary both pitch and rhythm by going up and down by one step with different note values.

These are steps:

Find steps and repeated notes:

6

LESSON II

New note: 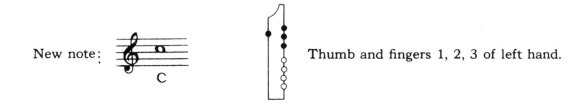 Thumb and fingers 1, 2, 3 of left hand.

C

Now we have three notes:  in the key of C major

These notes are   1   2   3

This key is called C major because C is the "home tone". A melody may go on excursions away from home, but in the end it will come back.

Play several times; sing these patterns with their numbers:

1   2   3   3   2   1

Listen to the difference. Which pattern moves up? Which moves down?

Play several times; sing with numbers.

1   3   3   1

Notice that this pattern moves by a skip. Our first skip.

Here are some examples of variety with these three tones.

1. This melody moves by steps:

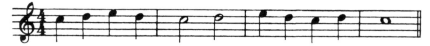

2. This melody moves by skips:

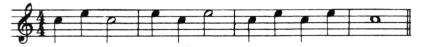

3. This melody moves by steps, skips and repeated notes:

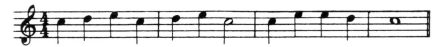

Here are some familiar tunes on these three tones.

Hot Cross Buns

Tune from "Au clair de la lune"

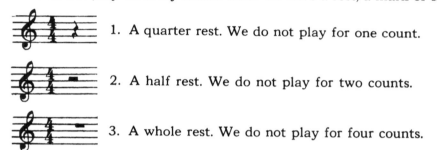

repeat sign

Sometimes we do not play on every count. Then we have a rest, a mark of silence.

1. A quarter rest. We do not play for one count.

2. A half rest. We do not play for two counts.

3. A whole rest. We do not play for four counts.

Now we put notes and rests together:

Count: 1 2 3 4 1 2 3 4 1 2 3 4 1 2 3 4

Make up other examples with notes and rests.

LESSON III

New Notes:

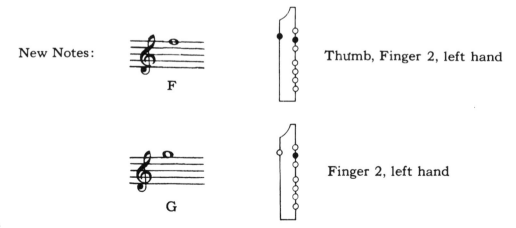

F — Thumb, Finger 2, left hand

G — Finger 2, left hand

Now we have five notes:

These notes are: 1   2   3   4   5   in the key of C major

Play several times and sing:

1 2 3 4   5   5 4 3 2   1   1 3 5   5 3 1

With five notes, many more skips are possible. Play and sing:

Skips from C:

Skips from D:

Skips from E:

Skips from F:

Skips from G:

(Note to teacher: *Do ear-training "guessing games" with skips.*)

Round

In a round, two or more people play the same song, starting at different points, indicated here by numbers. The song is played at least twice by everybody. The person who begins last ends the song alone.

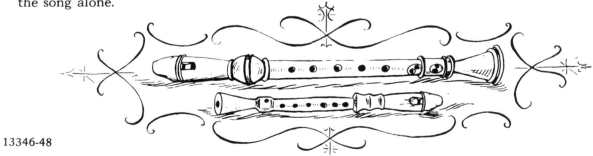

The Bee GERMAN

Go Tell Aunt Rhodie AMERICAN

Hansel and Gretel GERMAN

13346-48

May Song

GERMAN

LESSON IV

New time signature: means that we have three counts in each measure. Each count equals a quarter note or its equivalent.

Feel these rhythms; play on drum or other rhythmic instrument:

Make up rhythms, mixing the above patterns.

Example:

Choose the rhythm you like best and make up a melody on the five notes you have learned.
Remember you may step or skip.

Example:

Fais Do Do

FRENCH

Cuckoo

GERMAN

Green Gravel

ENGLISH

Beware

GERMAN

Note that this song starts on the last beat of the measure instead of the first. This last beat is called an upbeat.

Two Dance Tunes

18TH CENTURY

LESSON V

New note value. Eighth note:  Eighth rest:

Two eighth notes equal one quarter note. How many eighth notes equal a half note? A whole note?

Clap, play on drum or other rhythmic instrument:

Let's see what happens when we put the eighth notes on different beats of the measure:

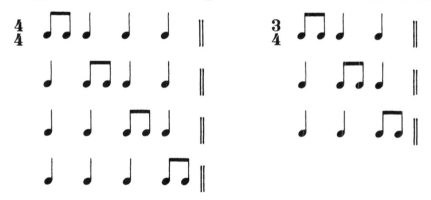

1. Make up rhythms in $\frac{4}{4}$ and $\frac{3}{4}$ time using some eighth notes.

Examples:

13346-48

2. Choose the rhythms you like best and make up melodies on the five notes you have learned.

Examples:.

Folk Song   GERMAN

Round

Winter, Good Bye   GERMAN

Folk Song

GERMAN

Silesian Folk Song

GERMAN

LESSON VI

New time signature: means that we have two counts in each measure and each count equals a quarter note or its equivalent.

13346-48

Clap; play on drum. Feel the strong (down) beat.

Make up rhythms of four measures each, mixing the above rhythmic patterns. Choose the ones you like best and make up melodies on the five notes you have learned.

Example:

Cradle Song　　　　　　　　　　　　　　　　　　　ROUSSEAU

New notes:

B

B flat

Thumb, fingers 1,2,3 left hand; fingers 2,3,4 right hand. *(German)*

Thumb, fingers 1,2,3 left hand; fingers 2, 3, right hand. *(English)*

Thumb, fingers 1,2,3 left hand; finger 1 right hand. *(German)*

Thumb, fingers 1,2,3 left hand; fingers 1,3,4 right hand. *(English)*

13346-48

Play:  Listen to the difference; B flat is a half tone lower than B.

Donkey Round (*3 part*) GERMAN

Run Ye Shepherds SILESIAN CHRISTMAS SONG

Folk Dance AUSTRIAN

13346-48

18

Here is a melody you learned in *LESSON IV* with an added accompaniment.

Fais Do Do

LESSON VII

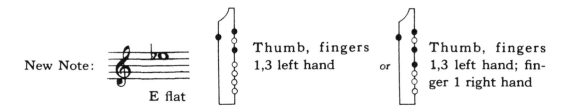

New Note:

E flat

Thumb, fingers 1,3 left hand   or   Thumb, fingers 1,3 left hand; finger 1 right hand

These notes are:

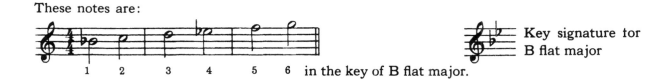

1   2   3   4   5   6   in the key of B flat major.

Key signature for B flat major

In B flat major, our key signature tells us that we must play *E flat* (♭) instead of *E natural* (♮) throughout the piece, unless otherwise indicated.

Write, play and sing the skips from 1, 2, 3, 4, 5, 6 of B flat major as we did in *LESSON II* from C.

Game Song

GERMAN

Round

Shepherd's Call

BOHEMIAN

20

Round

GERMAN

Twinkle, Twinkle, Little Star

Folk Song

16TH CENTURY GERMAN

13346-48

We can now play all our songs in this new key—B flat major. Putting a song from one key into another key is called transposition. Let us transpose "Hot Cross Buns" from C to B flat major.

First, we find our new home tone—B flat. The song begins on tone 3. In the new key of B flat major, tone 3 is D. We move down a step to C, another step down to B flat. This pattern is repeated in the third and fourth measures. The fifth measure has four repeated quarter notes on tone 1 (home tone), and the sixth measure four repeated quarter notes on step up, on tone 2, which is C; the seventh and eighth measures are exactly like measures one and two.

Now transpose "Au clair de la lune" from C to B flat major.

Play the songs of *LESSONS V* and *VI* in the key of B flat major. Note on which number of the key each one starts. This is the way to find out on which tone to start in a new key.

These notes are:

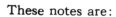

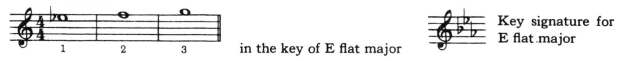

in the key of E flat major Key signature for E flat major

Play "Hot Cross Buns" and "Au claire de la lune" (first section) in the key of E flat major.

Whence, Oh Shepherd Maiden

FRENCH CAROL, 17TH CENTURY

13346-48

LESSON VIII

New symbol:  or

This is a tie. When two notes of the same pitch are connected with a tie, they are played as one note.

When you see a dot placed after a note, you add to that note one-half its value.

Examples:

Clap, then play these rhythms on percussion instruments:

Merrily We Roll Along

Play in B flat major.

Children's Song from the Rhineland

13346-48

Susie, Little Susie

GERMAN FOLK SONG

Steal Away ·

GERMAN

Fine

D. C. al Fine

Here is a familiar song:

May Song GERMAN

Let us change this song by making the first quarter note in each measure a dotted quarter note. Note other necessary changes:

LESSON IX

New symbol: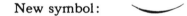

 This is a slur. When two or more notes of different pitch are connected with a slur, only the first note is tongued. This is called legato playing.

Play these examples in the different ways indicated. Listen carefully for the difference.

(T = tongued)·

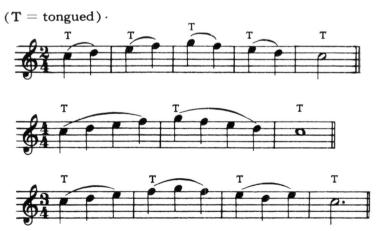

13346-48

Lullaby

Fine

D. C. al Fine

Eia Popeia

Sleep, Baby Sleep GERMAN

Dormi, dormi bel bambin ITALIAN LULLABY

13346-48

LESSON X

New notes:

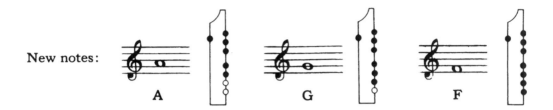

Notice that you have now added fingers 2, 3 and 4 of your right hand.

These notes are:

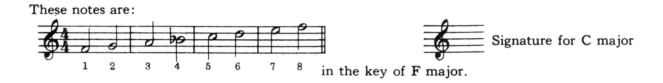

1 2 3 4 5 6 7 8   in the key of **F** major.

Signature for C major

This is our first complete scale. Play and sing up and down.

Write in your music notebook, play and sing the skips from 1, 2, 3, 4, 5, 6, 7, 8 of **F** major.

Choose several of your favorite songs and transpose them into the key of **F** major.

These notes are:

5 6 7 8 2 3 4 5   in the key of **B** flat major.

All the Birds

GERMAN

Hark, What's Coming from Outside

GERMAN

Can you find the part of the melody that appears first in eighth notes and is later repeated in quarter notes? Listen to the change from the movement in eighths to the movement in quarters and the change in mood that is expressed. This is a German folk song. In the first part a boy hears the steps of his sweetheart outside and expects her to come in. In the second part he says that she passed by but did not come in.

Swing Low, Sweet Chariot

NEGRO SPIRITUAL

Fine

D. C. al Fine

Christmas Nightingale

GERMAN

Come Ye Shepherds

BOHEMIAN

Satarello

16TH CENTURY ENGLISH

Three Rounds

GERMAN

Sometimes players of rounds stop at the same time. This is indicated by this sign ⌒

Look for a good folk song collection. You will find many songs that you can play. Some of them you may have to transpose into another key that better fits your range.

LESSON XI

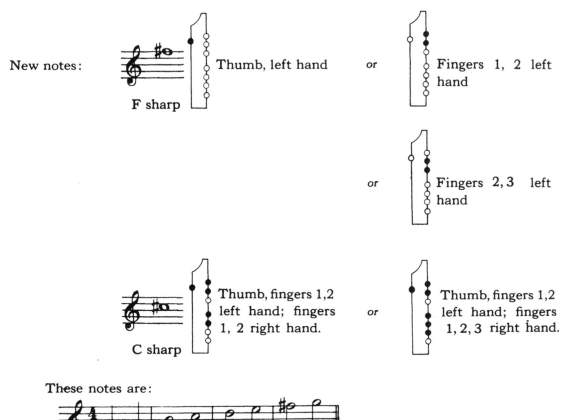

New notes:

F sharp — Thumb, left hand *or* Fingers 1, 2 left hand

or Fingers 2, 3 left hand

C sharp — Thumb, fingers 1,2 left hand; fingers 1, 2 right hand. *or* Thumb, fingers 1,2 left hand; fingers 1, 2, 3 right hand.

These notes are:

1 2 3 4 5 6 7 8 in the key of G major

Key signature for
G major

 means that we play F-sharp (instead of F-natural) throughout and the piece, unless otherwise indicated by the natural sign.

Oh, Rock-a My Soul   NEGRO SPIRITUAL

Fine

D. C. al Fine

Rounds

GERMAN

The Little Woman and the Peddler

ENGLISH

13346-48

These notes are:

in the key of D major

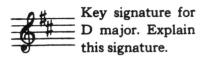

Key signature for D major. Explain this signature.

French Lullaby

These notes are:

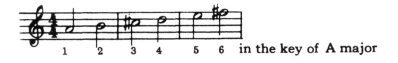

in the key of A major

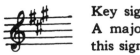

Key signature for A major. Explain this signature.

French Folk Song

Transpose:
1. "All the Birds" from *LESSON X* into the key of G major.
2. The pieces from *LESSON II* into the key of D major.
3. "Steal Away" from *LESSON VIII* into the key of A major.

Now is the Month of Maying

MORLEY

Serenade

HAYDN

Folk Song

GERMAN

LESSON XII

The Minor Key (Mode)

Our first key was C major

These notes are:

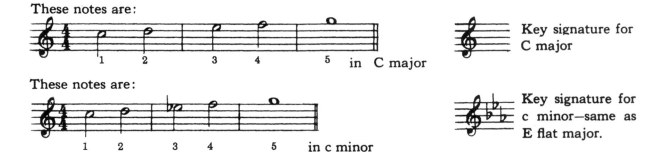

Write, play and sing the skips from 1,2,3,4,5 in c minor.

Play the song "Go Tell Aunt Rhodie" in the key of c minor.

We can now play in these minor keys:

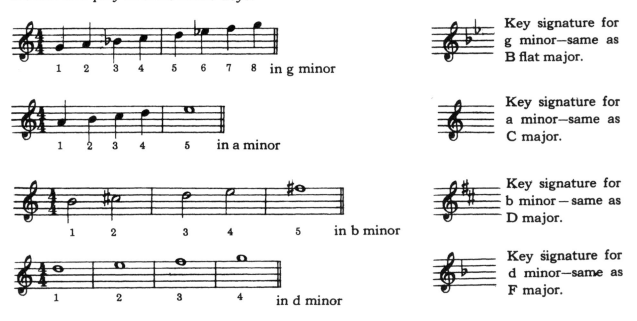

Morris Dance   ENGLISH

Good Night (*Round*) OLD ENGLISH

Maria's Dream 16TH CENTURY GERMAN

Flemish Song (*1540*)

The Turtle Dove ENGLISH

13346-48

A Round from Finland

Two Russian Folk Tunes

Bohemian Melody

Supplementary Material

Two Canons

Pater noster

ANONYMOUS, ABOUT 1550

GUMPELZHAIMER (1559-1625)

13346-48

Four Old Dances

1

In this piece you will find D flat. This means that the D is lowered a half step. It is played like C sharp. This is called an enharmonic exchange.

Soprano and Alto

IV

How Should I Your True Love Know (Elizabethan melody)

13346-48

Canon

QUIRSFELD (1642-1736)

Canon for Soprano and Alto

BORONI (18TH CENTURY)

Three Dances for 2 Recorders

PHILIPPE ESPRIT CHEDEVILLE (1684-1782)

Air

March

Air

III

Menuet

LULLY (1632-1687)

46

Two Melodies

Allegro

CORELLI

Menuet

The Little Sandman

GERMAN

Lo, How A Rose E'er Blooming

MELODY, 16TH CENTURY.
Harmonized by Praetorius

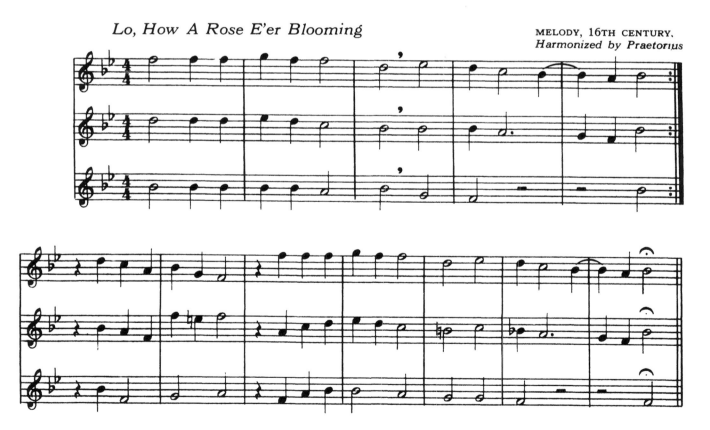

13346-48

From "The Magic Flute"

MOZART